The Beatles

The Beatles

by George Zanderbergen

Reprinted 1978

Library of Congress Catalog Card Number: 76-24211. International Standard Book Number: 0-913940-54-2.

Design - Doris Woods and Randal M. Heise

PHOTOGRAPHIC CREDITS

The illustration of this book was made possible through the cooperation of:

Capital Records and Wide World Photos.

The Beatles

Beatlemania

It was new! It was wild! It was weird!

It was staid, old Carnegie Hall — the place in New York where classical musicians played. But not on this day. Not on February 12, 1964.

There was music being made that day. Four young musicians were on the stage. Three of them played guitars and the fourth played the drums. Their music was loud. It came thundering out of electric amplifiers.

Even so — it was drowned out by the screams of the fans!

Thousands of teenagers packed Carnegie Hall. They squealed and groaned and howled and stamped their feet until the old building shook. Outside, crowds of young people who could not get in were kept orderly by New York policemen.

The sign on Carnegie Hall told New Yorkers who the musicians were. It said:

THE BEATLES

Puzzled adults stared at the sign. "Who are the Beatles?" they asked. "What are the Beatles?"

They would soon find out.

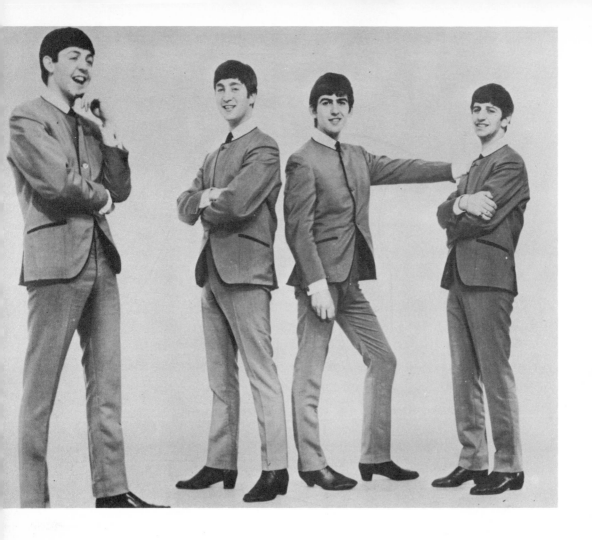

The Beatles sort of snuck up on America. They were from England, where they had been a big success. Their records had sold by the millions. They had played for British royalty.

But at first, their records flopped in the U.S.A.

The Beatles announced that they would tour America. A large record company took them on and pushed their records. By January 1964, one of their songs was Number 1 on the sales charts.

It was "I Want to Hold Your Hand."

It was a funny kind of rock song. Most American rock in those days had a downbeat message. It was sad or loud and driving and crude. The words were heavy and the tunes were simple-minded.

The Beatle song was different. It was cheery, but it still had a powerful rock beat. The tune was tricky — and if you hummed it, you found that the melody was one that you remembered.

And you remembered the Beatles themselves!

Beatles arrive at San Francisco International Airport for an American tour.

America first got to know them when the group appeared on a popular TV program, "The Ed Sullivan Show." Some 73 million people watched the show that night. They saw four very young men dressed in tight gray suits without lapels.

And they had long hair.

In the early 1960's, most young men wore crew cuts. Oh, some had greasy ducktail hairdos, but they were the rebels.

The Beatles pose for press photographers with TV personality Ed Sullivan.

But here were the Beatles, with their hair combed down in bangs over their foreheads, and brushing their tall collars in the back. The Beatles didn't look dangerous. They looked odd, but cute. They wiggled when they played and sang, but they were not like Elvis Presley, who was then King of Rock in America.

Young American girls who had not liked Elvis decided that they adored the Beatles. They flocked to Beatle concerts, and bought millions of Beatle records.

Wherever the Beatles played, huge crowds gathered. The fans screamed and fainted. It was a new kind of madness — **Beatlemania.**

Stores sold Beatle buttons and Beatle wigs and Beatle dolls. Pictures of the Beatles peered from every magazine. Their songs crowded others off the airwaves. Everywhere you went, you heard **"She Loves You," "Please Please Me," "Do You Want to Know a Secret,"** and **"Can't Buy Me Love."**

Parents who had sneered at other rock music didn't seem to mind the Beatles so much. Why? Well it was hard to say. The Beatles were certainly loud. But they weren't scary or grim, as some other rock stars were.

So young people were allowed to go to Beatle concerts and buy Beatle records. Overflow crowds greeted the young Englishmen on their American tour. They attracted more fans than any show business people in history.

They became a legend.

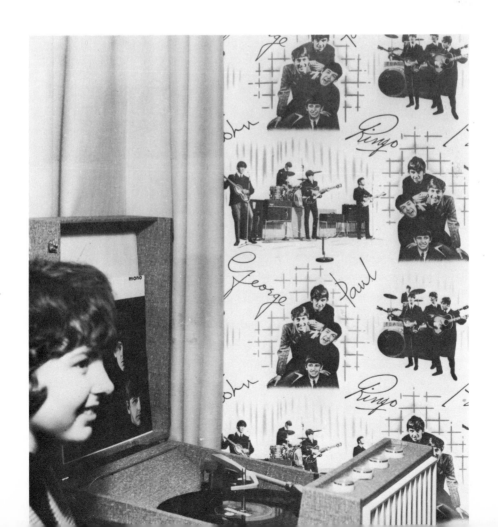

The Beatles made a movie. It was called **A Hard Day's Night.** Film critics went to see the movie and prepared to sneer. They thought it would be just another teenage song-and-dance movie.

But **A Hard Day's Night** was different. The clever director, Richard Lester, let the Beatles make fun of themselves. They kidded the whole rock scene. The movie was full of wildly funny moments. It was something like an old-time silent comedy in parts, with action going on while Beatle music played in the background.

Serious music critics decided that **A Hard Day's Night** was a little gem. Kids just thought it was fun. The movie helped make the Beatles more popular than ever.

Songs from the movie became instant classics. There was the lively title tune, of course. But the best melodies were two love ballads — **"And I Love Her"** and **"If I Fell."** They were enjoyed by adults as well as by teenagers. Even the Boston Pops Orchestra made a record of Beatle songs!

The Beatles made another movie, **"Help!"** It was not as artistic as **Hard Day's** but it had a wide appeal. It was full of crazy chase scenes and slapstick humor. It made the Beatles seem like innocent, fun-loving young boys, who just happened to be caught up in strange adventures.

And that was the image they had in America.

Not everybody liked the Beatles.

Old-fashioned folk looked with horror upon their "long" hair. It was a threat to familiar American lifestyles.

Other people thought the heavy beat and loud sound of their music was somehow sinful. These people could hardly wait for Beatlemania to fade away.

In June 1965, Queen Elizabeth gave the four Beatles special medals. They were made Members of the Most Excellent Order of the British Empire. Stuffy

Englishmen were horrified. How could the Queen do such a thing?

She did it because the Beatles' record sales brought needed money to Britain.

The Beatles kept their faces straight when they met the Queen. But later on, they laughed and laughed. Getting the honor was such a good joke on the world. Statesmen and heroes and great actors had received the MBE. But Beatles!

Why, they were just four lads from the slums of Liverpool. Four lads who struck it lucky . . . .

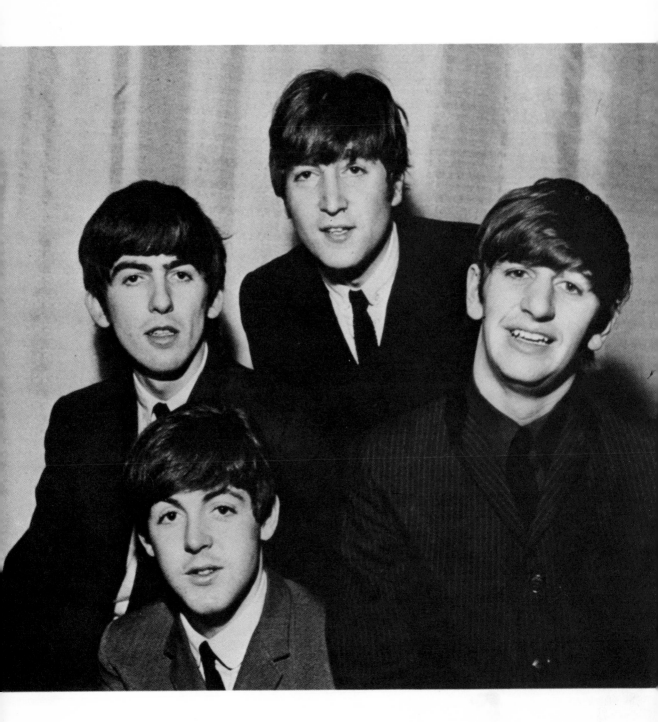

The Boys from Liverpool

Liverpool is a very large city in the North of England. It is a shipping center, and has many factories. The people who live there are mostly poor and hard-working.

John Lennon, "Beatle-in-Chief," was born in Liverpool in 1940. Britain was at war. Little John came into the world during an air raid.

His father, Alfred Lennon, was away at sea. He worked as a waiter on a steamship. His mother, Julia, was a gay witty woman who liked to sing and have a good time. She didn't seem to have much time for her baby boy.

The war kept Alfred and Julia Lennon apart. They stopped caring for each other and separated. Julia's sister, Mimi, begged to keep the baby. Julia agreed that it was probably best for John.

Mimi and her husband, George, tried to make a loving home for John. But he was a difficult child. He was full of fun and loved his aunt, but he always seemed to get into trouble.

He fought. He stole things. His schoolwork was poor. Still — he might have straightened out. But then his mother came back. She lived not far from Mimi's house. Whenever Mimi was strict with John, he would run away to his mother's place.

Julia was a fun-loving rebel. She did not really know what was good for a young boy. He needed a firm hand. But she encouraged him to enjoy himself. She mocked John's teachers. She didn't mind when the 13-year-old boy smoked and drank.

John liked to play the guitar at school. Mimi thought this was a waste of time — but Julia didn't. She got him a secondhand guitar. John practiced and tried to imitate Elvis Presley's style. He and some friends from Quarry School formed a little band. They called themselves the Quarrymen. John was the leader.

And that was the start of it, in 1956.

In June of that year, the Quarrymen were playing at a church party. They were a "skiffle" band, making a loud, cheerful noise without much real talent.

When the set was over, a young boy came to talk to the Quarrymen. He borrowed a guitar and played **"Twenty Flight Rock."** It was a tough tune, but the kid did a good job. In fact, he was a lot better than any of the Quarrymen!

John Lennon wondered if he should invite the kid to join the band. The boy said goodbye and left the church, but John Lennon remembered his name.

Paul McCartney.

Paul was born in Liverpool in 1942. His father, Jim McCartney, had a little ragtime band when he was young. Later he became a cotton salesman. Paul's mother, Mary Patricia, was a nurse.

Paul was the first McCartney child. He had a younger brother named Michael. When he was young, Paul did very well in school. But when he was about 13, he began to get bored. Other boys in the neighborhood made fun of his high grades and his rather chubby face. They called Paul "college pudding." He hated that, so he began to do poor work on purpose.

The boys that Paul admired most were tough. So he decided he would be tough, too. The loud, wicked beat of rock 'n' roll music appealed to him. He began to play the guitar, trying to imitate Elvis Presley and Little Richard.

When Paul was 14, his mother died of cancer. The boy was crushed by grief. He turned more and more to music in order to forget his sorrow. He practiced until he was very good on the guitar. He also composed a few songs of his own.

And then he met John Lennon.

When the two future Beatles met in 1956, John was 16 and Paul was 14. They became friends very quickly. Both boys were rebels. Both loved rock 'n' roll music. Both had a crazy sense of humor.

They entered a talent contest and called themselves the "British Everly Brothers." They won first prize.

Paul was invited to join the Quarrymen. Two other boys got tired of playing in the group and dropped out. Paul said he knew a friend from school who was good on the guitar. He was only 13, but he could play **"Guitar Boogie Shuffle"** all the way through!

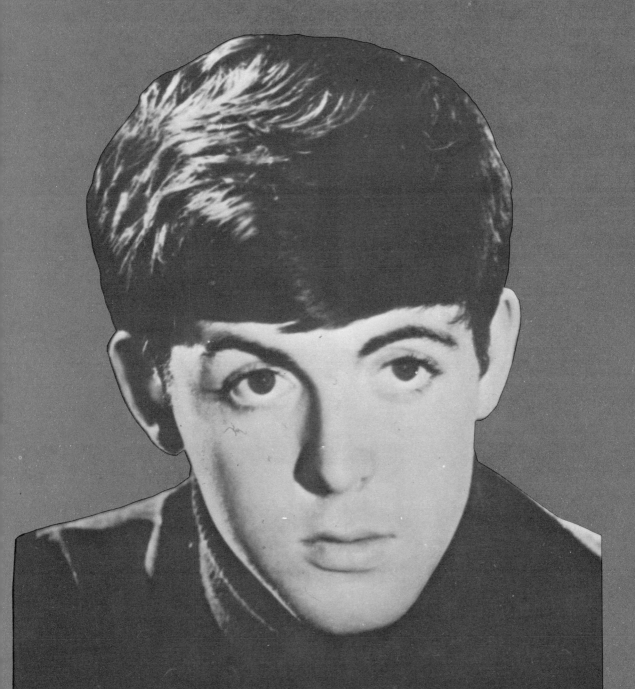

PAUL McCARTNEY

So George Harrison came onto the scene.

George was born in Liverpool in 1943. He was the youngest of the four children of Harold and Louise Harrison. His father was a bus driver. His mother loved music and taught a dancing class in her spare time.

Young George found schoolwork to be so easy that it bored him. He wanted to stand out from the other boys, so he took to wearing flashy clothes. The teachers disapproved, and this made George feel good!

George decided to learn to play the guitar when he was about 12. At first, he was very bad. "I'll never make it, Mum!" he moaned. His mother urged him to keep trying. When he finally learned to play well, she got him an expensive electric guitar.

Paul McCartney often came to George's house to practice. When Paul introduced George to John Lennon, all three boys began coming to the Harrison home. Mrs. Harrison liked to keep an eye on them.

Then something awful happened. John's mother Julia, was struck by a car and killed. Her death tore poor John apart. He had been going to art school, but he was not doing well. The only thing that kept him from going crazy was his music.

John, Paul, and George began to change from amateur musicians to semi-pros in 1958. They played at a teenage "cellar club" called the Casbah. They earned small amounts of money and slowly decided that their best chances for the future lay in becoming professionals.

The Birth

of the Beatles

Other boys came and went in the little rock group. But John, Paul, and George stuck together. The group had many different names. First they were the Quarreymen, then the Rainbows, then Johnny and the Moondogs. In 1959, John admired a group called Buddy Holly and the Crickets. It started him thinking about bugs.

How about **Beetles?** How about **Beatles,** to go with beatniks and beat music? Finally, the group called itself the Silver Beatles. They were hired for a two-week tour of Scotland — and they were a success!

Then they returned to the Casbah, where they attracted large crowds. Among the people who came to listen was the owner of a night club in Hamburg, Germany. At that time, German young people were wild about Liverpool-style rock. The night-club man invited the Beatles to come to Hamburg. He offered them a salary that seemed very large.

The boys' families tried to keep them at home. But at last, John, Paul, George, and a drummer named Pete Best left England. It was 1960. History was about to be made.

The German night club was a crummy, run-down place. But the Beatles made it jump with their loud rock music. They wore tight jeans, pointy-toe shoes, black leather jackets, and greasy Elvis Presley hair styles.

The main thing they learned in Germany was to play very, very loudly. Otherwise they couldn't be heard over the din of the crowd. They also cut some records, which didn't sell too well.

When the Beatles came back from Germany, they discovered that they were playing a different kind of music from the other Liverpool groups. Their sound was new, more exciting, more primitive. A second trip to Germany in 1961 firmed the new style. When they came home, they played to packed houses.

One day in 1961, a customer came into a large Liverpool record store, and asked for one of the German-made Beatle records. The owner of the store, 27-year-old Brian Epstein, had never heard of the group. But he decided to find out about them.

Brian went to the Cavern, a club where the Beatles were packing them in. He was fascinated by the new style of music. After a few weeks, he convinced the boys that he could make them stars. He wanted to become the Beatles' manager.

The Beatles agreed. They were impressed by Brian's contacts in the record business. They auditioned for a large record company, Decca. And they were turned down. But a smaller company, Parlophone, agreed to put out a Beatle disc.

Beatles with manager Brian Epstein, (far left) 1965.

John, Paul, and George were overjoyed. But they had one problem. They did not like Pete Best's style of drumming. Best was handsome and had a lot of fans. But his beat was crude. The three boys told Brian Epstein that they wanted him to fire Pete Best. They wanted another drummer.

They wanted Ringo Starr.

Ringo's real name was Richard Starkey. He was born in Liverpool in 1940, the son of Richard and Elsie Starkey. When little Ritchie was 3, his parents separated. His mother went to work as a barmaid, while the boy stayed with his grandmother.

When he was 6, Ritchie became very sick. He had appendix trouble and had to stay in the hospital for a whole year. He fell behind in school. But a kind young girl, who became his babysitter, taught him to read and write.

At the age of 13, Ritchie was sick again — this time with a lung disease. He had to spend two more years in the hospital. There was a little band in his ward, and Ritchie liked to play the drum.

When Ritchie got out of the hospital, it was time for him to learn a trade. But he did poorly at most of the things he tried. He joined a skiffle band at work. And his stepfather, Harry Graves, bought him a cheap set of drums.

Ritchie practiced hard. His grandfather helped him to buy a better set of drums later on. It took a whole year for Ritchie to pay his grandfather back.

Ritchie played in small rock groups, much as the other three Beatles had, and kept on with his regular job as well. But then he had a chance to play full-time with a group called Rory Storme and the Hurricanes. He quit his job and became a drummer. By the time he was 21, in 1961, the Hurricanes were doing well.

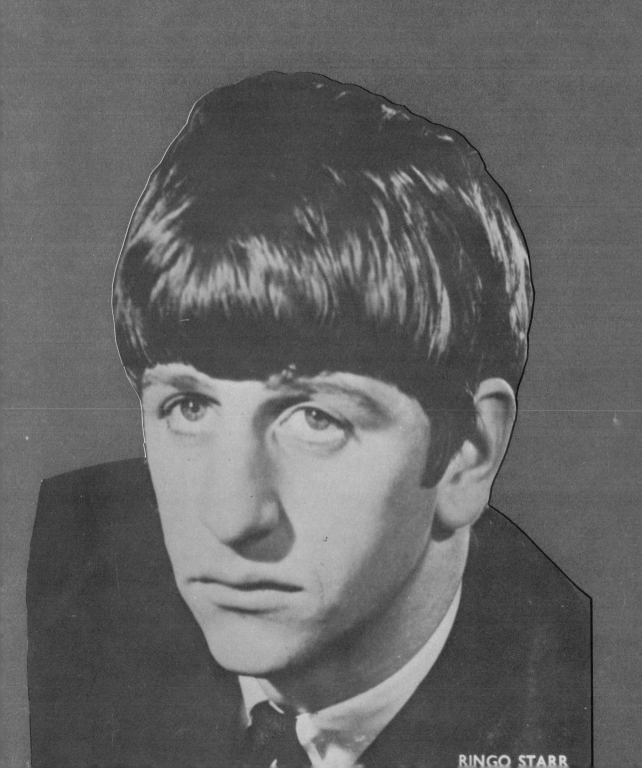

RINGO STARR

Like the Beatles, the Hurricanes went to Hamburg. (And they learned to imitate the Beatle style!) When they returned to England, they became one of the most popular rock groups in Liverpool.

By then, Ritchie Starkey had become Ringo Starr. He liked to wear lots of rings while he played. All of the other musicians liked Ringo. He was not only a good drummer, but he was also a friendly, good-humored lad. The Beatles met him in Hamburg and were impressed with his talent and his personality.

Ringo joined the group just before they made their first record for Parlophone. It featured two Lennon-McCartney songs — **"Love Me, Do"** and **"PS, I Love You,"** The record reached Number 17 on the charts.

Another record, **"Please Please Me,"** came out in January 1963. It made Number 1!

Brian Epstein had changed the Beatles' image not long after he took over as manager. Gone were the leather jackets and the greased-down hair. The Beatles who toured England early in 1963 had neat suits with ties and vests. Their hair was ungreasy and combed over the forehead in bangs. This style was popular in Europe at the time; but it was very new in England. It helped make the Beatles different.

At first, they were popular only in Liverpool. But then their fame began to spread. Larger and larger crowds greeted them on tour. They cut an album, and it quickly sold out.

In October, they played at the huge London Palladium theater. The show was televised all over England, and it was a smash success. When the Beatles tried to leave the theatre, they were met by a mob of thousands of screaming girls. The fans almost crushed the Beatles, before the boys escaped in their car!

George and John are mobbed in Dallas during a 1964 concert.

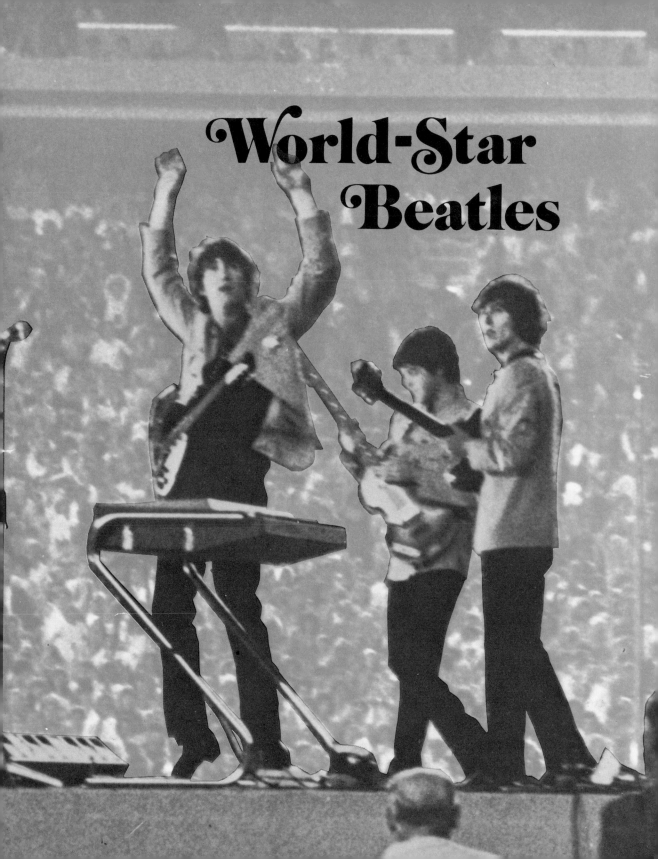

World-Star Beatles

England had never known anything like it. The mob scene made the front pages of the papers. The publicity caused more and more fans to buy records and come to Beatle concerts.

And in November, they were invited to perform before the royal family, The Queen Mother, Princess Margaret, and Lord Snowdon. The Beatles did **"She Loves You," "Till There Was You,"** and **"Twist and Shout."**

John asked the crowd to clap in time to the music. Then he turned to the royal box and said: "Those upstairs, just rattle your jewelry!"

The gentle joke was the talk of England.

By the end of 1963, the Beatles were voted the top musical group in England. Their singles, **"She Loves You"** and **"I Want to Hold Your Hand"** had sold more than a million apiece. The Beatles were popular not only as performers, but also as composers. One serious British music critic even said:

"They are the greatest composers since Beethoven."

In the midst of all this adoration, the Beatles kept their sense of humor. They disarmed hostile reporters with their comical remarks. They made fun of their own success.

And they kept on singing, playing, and composing.

There was a Beatle for every taste. John was the deep thinker. He wrote two strange books — **In His Own Write** and **Spaniard in the Works.** Critics did not understand them, so people decided the books must be good!

Paul was the clean-cut, adorable Beatle. Girls felt he was singing just for them. The more sentimental Beatle songs were mostly his work.

George was the shy, mysterious Beatle. People would get him mixed up with John or Paul. He looked sad and moody, and fans decided they wanted to mother him and cheer him up.

And Ringo! In America, he was the most popular Beatle of all. His big nose and small, skinny body set him apart from the others. He was something like a lovable puppy — clumsy, eager to please, full of gentle humor and wistful friendliness. He was the star of the second Beatle movie, **"Help!"**

At the end of 1965, it seemed that the Beatle craze might finally be fading out. The boys were tired of the mobs and the screaming that followed them on tour. John and Ringo were married and George wanted to get married, too. But the girl fans pestered the Beatle wives, and even threatened them! The dark side of being famous began to eat at the Beatles — especially John.

In late 1965, their album **"Rubber Soul"** came out. It had two splendid, unusual songs — **"Michelle"** and **"Norwegian Wood."** In the latter, George played the sitar — a stringed instrument from India. It gave the song a spooky, remote quality. The words were spooky, too. The two young people in the song were strangely out of tune.

The Beatles made their last British tour in 1965 and planned their last American tour for summer 1966. Meanwhile, their **"Revolver"** album came out. Some of its songs were very striking. They were far different from the simple melodies of other rock composers. And many of the lyrics were as deeply thoughtful as poems. **"Eleanor Rigby"** was a tale of loneliness. **"Taxman"** was a bitter dig at the British government. **"Doctor Robert"** had a pill to cure any trouble. **"Yellow Submarine"** was a child's trip away from the cruel world of reality.

The Beatles were saying things about themselves. They had become more than entertainers. They wanted to talk about what was wrong with the world, wrong with peoples' lives, what was true, and what was false.

In the middle 1960's, this was an unusual thing for pop singers to do.

Suddenly, the Beatles were no longer cute little plastic people. They admitted that fame troubled them. They also admitted that they had taken drugs, to try to escape from tension and unhappiness. Two songs, **"Strawberry Fields Forever"** and **"Penny Lane"** are descriptions of drug trips.

The 1967 album, **"Sgt. Pepper's Lonely Hearts Club Band"** had two drug songs, too — **"A Little Help From My Friends"** and **"Lucy in the Sky with Diamonds."** But, by then, the Beatles had discovered that drugs were no real answer to human problems.

They began to look elsewhere.

They investigated religion. The simple Christianity of lower-class Britain did not appeal to them. Once,

John pointed out disgustedly, "The Beatles are more popular than Jesus Christ now."

They told Brian Epstein they would be making no more tours after 1966. They wanted to dig more deeply into their music and into their private soul-searching.

Brian, who had guided the Beatles into world-stardom, was suddenly cast adrift. He did not understand what the Beatles were trying to say in the **"Sgt. Pepper"** album, which received enormous acclaim from serious music critics.

Once the Beatles had leaned on Brian. Now they no longer needed him. One day, he accidentally took too many sleeping pills, and died.

"It's like the end of a chapter," said George.

Twilight and New Dawn

George was the first Beatle to take up Eastern religion. He went to India to study the sitar. There he met an Indian guru, or holy man. George was excited by the guru's teachings. He told the other Beatles about his experience, when they got together to make **"Sgt. Pepper."**

A guru named the Maharishi Mahesh Yogi came to England. The Beatles became followers of his. They decided to go with him to India and become mystics. They thought they would find happiness by giving up the comfortable life and thinking beautiful thoughts.

George enjoyed the experience. But not the other three Beatles. They got tired of meditating, and decided to search for truth somewhere else.

In 1968, the Beatles were featured in a cartoon movie, **Yellow Submarine.** It was a big hit in America. They released several more albums. Their best song was **"Hey Jude."**

But the Beatles were growing older — and growing apart. John had married a girl from his art school, Cynthia Powell, in 1963. They were divorced in 1968, and John married a Japanese artist, named Yoko Ono, the following year. The other Beatles never got along well with Yoko. She had far-out ideas that alarmed Paul and his new wife, Linda Eastman.

George Harrison performs at Bengla Desh benefit. His friends are Bob Dylan and Leon Russell.

In 1970, the Beatles made their last album, **"Let It Be."** They also made a film with the same title, showing them at work. They argue a lot in the movie as they put together the songs for the album. You can tell that they no longer think the same way about their music. But at the end, they forget their squabbles and do a concert on the roof above a busy city street. The people stop to listen and cause a traffic jam.

The movie seemed to say several things. It showed that the Beatles were growing apart. It showed the great problems that face four Liverpool lads suddenly become millionaire businessmen. And it showed that the Beatles — for all their dislike of screeching fans — still wanted crowds of people to listen to their music.

But not just young people. All kinds of people.

After **"Let It Be,"** the Beatles pursued separate careers. John and Yoko went to live in America, where they protested the Vietnam War and made some albums together.

George went deeper and deeper into his Indian music. He made a successful album, **"All Things Must Pass."** And in 1971, he helped put together a great concert in Madison Square Garden. It was a benefit for the starving people of Bangla Desh. George and Ringo played, and so did Bob Dylan. There were also other rock stars, and Indian musicians, such as Ravi Shankar and Ali Akhbar Khan.

Meanwhile, Ringo played in several movies. He also made albums on his own — and many of them were hits. But his 10-year marriage to a Liverpool girl, Maureen Cox, broke up in 1975. Not even peaceful Ringo was the man he used to be. None of them were. The lyrics of **"Yesterday"** were coming true for the Beatles.

Paul McCartney cut himself completely off from the other three Beatles. He tried to break the contract that bound the group together. He made albums on his own, with his wife Linda, and with his new group, **Wings.** At first, Paul's efforts were not a success. His songs were called "too sweet" or "too commercial."

But in 1974, all that changed. Wings' album **"Band on the Run"** was a huge best-seller. And the 1975 Wings disc, **"Venus and Mars,"** did just as well. Paul's new songs were middle-of-the-road pop. But they were excellent pop and they found a large audience.

By 1976, Paul's Wings was one of the hottest musical groups in the world.

So each of the four Beatles built a new career for himself. Each found success on his own, with different kinds of music that appealed to different listeners.

46

Paul McCartney and his band, "Wings".

And at the same time that the new Beatles settled down, the old Beatles returned!

In 1976, many of the old Beatle numbers were re-issued. Songs such as **"Hey Jude"** and **"Yesterday"** climbed to the top of popularity charts.

For years, people had pleaded with the Beatles to get together again. That hadn't happened. But the songs they had sung together in the 1960's were a very important part of musical history. They would not be forgotten. The Beatles helped change the thinking of the world. Through them, the youth culture was able to motivate adults for the first time in history.

It was a weird thing. It was a wonderful thing. And all done with music.